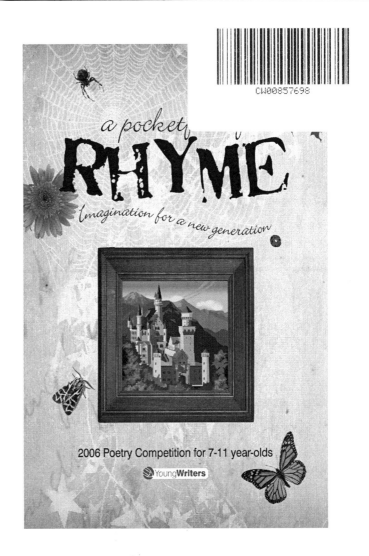

a pocket

RHYME

Imagination for a new generation

2006 Poetry Competition for 7-11 year-olds

Young**Writers**

Co Durham Vol I
Edited by Mark Richardson

 Young**Writers**

First published in Great Britain in 2006 by:
Young Writers
Remus House
Coltsfoot Drive
Peterborough
PE2 9JX
Telephone: 01733 890066
Website: www.youngwriters.co.uk

SB ISBN 1 84602 466 8

Foreword

Young Writers was established in 1991 and has been passionately devoted to the promotion of reading and writing in children and young adults ever since. The quest continues today. Young Writers remains as committed to the nurturing of poetic and literary talent as ever.

This year's Young Writers competition has proven as vibrant and dynamic as ever and we are delighted to present a showcase of the best poetry from across the UK and in some cases overseas. Each poem has been selected from a wealth of *A Pocketful Of Rhyme* entries before ultimately being published in this, our fourteenth primary school poetry series.

Once again, we have been supremely impressed by the overall quality of the entries we have received. The imagination, energy and creativity which has gone into each young writer's entry made choosing the poems a challenging and often difficult but ultimately hugely rewarding task - the general high standard of the work submitted ensured this opportunity to bring their poetry to a larger appreciative audience.

We sincerely hope you are pleased with this final collection and that you will enjoy *A Pocketful Of Rhyme Co Durham Vol I* for many years to come.

Contents

Delves Lane Junior School, Consett

Joanne Nixon (9)   1
Chloe Heighway (7)   2
Sophie Mawson (7)   3
Connor Coleman (9)   4
Gayle Craig (9)   5
Andrew Larmouth (10)   6
Rhiannon Turner (10)   7
Lauren Harrison (10)   8
Gareth Symonds (10)   9
Thomas McAloon (10)   10
Kieron Johnson (10)   11
Conor Metcalfe (10)   12
Leona Wilson (7)   13
Anna Eland (8)   14
Courtney Clark (10)   15
Kyle Routledge (10)   16
Kate McGuigan (10)   17
Connor Robinson (9)   18
Lauren East (10)   19
Autumn Colgrave (9)   20
Deanna Elliott (9)   21
Bethany Smith (10)   22
Frances Boyle (10)   23
Chloe Bell (8)   24
Georgia Bowman (9)   25
Charlotte Colgrave (7)   26
Bryce Freeman (9)   27
Abbie Ross (7)   28
Jemma Whaley (7)   29
Louise Brown (7)   30
Dana Dixon (9)   31
Alyce Carter (8)   32
Matthew Lamb (9)   33
Ethan Waller (8)   34
Thomas Ryan (10)   35
Dylan Elsdon (9)   36
Nico Jeffrey (10)   37
Chantelle Bessford (10)   38

Kieran Whitwood (10)   39
Connor Balmer (10)   40
Jordan Gibson (10)   41
Daniel Farthing (8)   42

Easington Colliery Primary School, Peterlee

Ashley Parkin (11)   43
Hannah Cook (11)   44
Scott Wardle (10)   45
Sean Fish (11)   46
Sophie Carr (10)   47
Meghan Robson (11)   48
Arron Musgrove (11)   49
James Johnson (10)   50
Carl Price (11)   51
Amy-Leigh McAndrew (11)   52
Natalie Carr (11)   53
Steven Pearce (11)   54
Shannon Stobbs (10)   55
Alice Marshall (10)   56
Robert Longstaff (11)   57
Chariti Boland (11)   58
Samantha Emerson (10)   59
Daniel Williamson (11)   60
Jordan Robinson (11)   61
James Dunn (10)   62
Sarah Bainbridge (10)   63
Courtney Hornsby (11)   64
Lauren Stockdale (11)   65
Rebecca Jones (11)   66
Kyle Anderson (11)   67
Jennifer Creed (10)   68
Kieran Charlton (11)   69
Stephanie Kendall (10)   70
Lauren Murray (10)   71
Jonathan Humphries (11)   72
Katie Randall (10)   73
Andrew Duff (11)   74
John-Paul Purcell (11)   75
Ellie Robson (10)   76
Bethany Knight (10)   77

Sophie Houghton (10)	78
Kirsty Kell (11)	79
Joe Foster (11)	80
Marley Rollins (10)	81
Ryan Wade (11)	82
Jordan Scott (10)	83
Michael Bryce (10)	84
Sarah Walker (11)	85
Georgia Dawson (11)	86

Ingleton CE Primary School, Darlington

Thomas Brown (10)	87
Jennifer Stephenson (10)	88
Roger Dunn (9)	89
Dale Deary (9)	90
Lucinda Elliott (10)	91
William Forster (9)	92
Charlotte Payne (9)	93
Sally Robinson (9)	94
Libby Duffy (9)	95
Becky Duffy (11)	96
Rebecca Toms (10)	97
Connor Redgrave (11)	98
Matthew Simpson (11)	99
Phillip Dennis (9)	100
Edmund Clarke (10)	101
Christopher Parker (10)	102
Peter Forster (9)	103

Raventhorpe Preparatory School, Darlington

Jason Maguire (9)	104
Imogen Storey (10)	105
Laura Marriott (9)	106
Charlotte Whittaker (10)	107
Naomi Duncan (10)	108
Saffron Pickup (9)	109
William Richardson (9)	110
Tom Knox (9)	111
Andrew Smith (10)	112
Chelsey Peart (10)	113
Grace Wray (10)	114

St Joseph's RC Primary School, Durham

Judith Langridge (10)   115
Sarah Edwards (10)   116

St Mary's Primary School, Consett

Lucy Phillips (8)   117
Sally O'Keeffe (9)   118
Abbey Thompson (8)   119
Jonathan Gorman (8)   120
Jasmine Urwin-Collier (9)   121
Hope Anderson (8)   122
James Donnelly (9)   123
Beth Palmer (9)   124
Ashleigh Clarke (8)   125
Shannon Harrop (9)   126
Casey Beard (9)   127
Anna McClen (9)   128
Richard Robinson (8)   129
Megan Grigg (9)   130
Laura Johnson (8)   131
Charlotte Cousin (9)   132
Laura Cassidy (9)   133
Anna Siddle (9)   134
Jordan Mitchell (9)   135
Michael Lilley (9)   136
Emily Phillips (9)   137
Charlotte Smith (9)   138
Anna Quinn (9)   139
Megan Birbeck (9)   140
Rebecca Swinney (9)   141
Sophie Milburn (9)   142
Gabrielle McAleer (11)   143
Roxanne Ives (11)   144
Anthony Brown (11)   145
Christopher Carlin (10)   146
Sophie Page (11)   147
Brandon Hicks (10)   148
Jayne Donnelly (11)   149
Susanna Quinn (10)   150
Emily Peacock (11)   151
Abbie Spence (10)   152

Caitlin O'Keeffe (11)	153
Katie Murphy (11)	154
Peter Leech (11)	155
Elizabeth Gibson (9)	156
Tom McClen (9)	157
Patrick Brown (9)	158
Hope Hilditch (9)	159
Aimee Simpson (9)	160
Hannah Roberts (9)	161
Katie Westgarth (9)	162
Adam Dent (9)	163
Hannah Phillips (11)	164
Rebecca Donnelly (11)	165
Lauren Parker (11)	166
Andrew Oates (11)	167
Robert Owens & Oliver Clarke (11)	168
Tom Malone & Jordan Donnellan (11)	169

St William's RC VA Primary School, Trimdon Station

Lucy Hannah Hudson (9)	170
Lauren Mayhew (9)	171
Rebecca Spellman (9)	172
Emeka Ononeze (9)	173
Jessica Storey (10)	174
Ciaran Jasper (10)	175
Aimee Elder (8)	176
Lorna Hubbard (9)	177
Sophie Fellows (10)	178
Sarah Cant (9)	179
Nicole Peters (11)	180
Vicky Barber (10)	181
James Slattery (10)	182
Megan Grimley (11)	183
Tom Robertson (10)	184
Abbie Geldard (10)	185
Terri Armstrong (11)	186
Jenny Harnett (9)	187
Shannon Turnbull (11)	188
Kallum James (11)	189
Matthew Butler (11)	190
Louise Gardiner (11)	191

Thomas Robertshaw (11) 192
Kyle Webb (11) 193
Thomas Barker (10) 194
Ryan Willis (10) 195
Rebecca Ashford (11) 196
Jordan Lavery (10) 197
Jane Snowball (10) 198
Claire Harnett (11) 199
Jessica Collett (9) 200
Robbie Morgan (9) 201

The Poems

You

You're like a groovy 60s and 70s night,
You're like a crunchy green salad on a summer's day,
You're like a blue wavy sea shining in the sunset,
You're a black swirl in my blackcurrant,
You're like Berwick's green field that I am playing in,
You're a happy smiley face on my good work,
You're like my black dog playing in the garden,
You're like a cold winter day with wind blowing in my face,
You're like a Sunday afternoon when my mum was holding me.

Joanne Nixon (9)
Delves Lane Junior School, Consett

My Sister

You're as gold as a summer morning.
You're like a delicious Sunday dinner.
You're as purple as a jewel.
You're like a cold orange juice in spring.
You're like the softest bit of fur.
You're as comfortable as my bed.
You make me happy every day.

Chloe Heighway (7)
Delves Lane Junior School, Consett

Kristy

You're like the sound of 'Hit Me Baby'.
You're as sweet as a McDonald's.
You're as red as a rose.
You're as creamy as a custard.
You're as soft as a ball of fluff.
You're as funny as my grandad.
You make me happy every day.

Sophie Mawson (7)
Delves Lane Junior School, Consett

My Mam

You're like the Black Eyed Peas singing their hit single.
You're like an irresistible juicy McChicken sandwich.
You're as beautiful as the glittering blue sea.
You're as tasty as 100 cans of Coke.
You're as cosy and comforting as wool.
You're as fun and exciting as Water World.
You're as fun-loving and caring as a fluffy doggy.
And that's Mam!

Connor Coleman (9)
Delves Lane Junior School, Consett

My Brother

You're like a crazy man at the trades dancing to my humps.
You're as skinny as a cheese and tomato pizza.
You're like a bubbling can of Coke.
You're as warm as a woolly jumper.
You're panting like a dog after football.
You're as happy as a tweeting bird
While I open my presents on my birthday.
You're my funny, playful, loving brother
And you always will be.

Gayle Craig (9)
Delves Lane Junior School, Consett

Tsunami Terror

A tsunami was heading to town,
That had a king who wore a crown.
Everyone who was on the sand,
Would run and wave their hand!
'Help, a tsunami is coming!'
People are running.
The king will help us,
But he has gone on a bus.
People swept away,
What a terrible day!

Andrew Larmouth (10)
Delves Lane Junior School, Consett

Disasters

Tornado swirling round the city, violently smashing and dragging cars.
Destructive roaring tornado, whirling powerfully.
The Earth begins to shake
Smell of smoke fills the air
All I can do is watch
The powerful tornado destroys our city.

Rhiannon Turner (10)
Delves Lane Junior School, Consett

Disasters

Tornado whirled around violently dragging more and more people to the aggressive whirl.

Buildings fell to the ground, windows shattered, people screaming for help.

Fear spread around the city, children clueless about what was happening.

The Devil has come!

Lauren Harrison (10)
Delves Lane Junior School, Consett

Disasters

Working by the light of my candle
The Earth starts to rumble, God has arisen from Heaven.
Looked out of the bedroom window, sky black like coal.
Streets riddled with corpses, cold wind gushing at my face.
The Earth will perish in fiery Hell.
Human life no more
Flashing lightning streaks
Madness in Manhattan
Chaos in California
Terror in Texas and deaths in Detroit.
The end of the world is nigh!

Gareth Symonds (10)
Delves Lane Junior School, Consett

Disaster

One day when I came home for a very important day
A tornado blew me a million miles away
My friend ended up in a massive cave
And then my friend saw a wave
My friend got washed away
My friend ended up in an earthquake
My friend got stuck with a bunch of snakes
To me he has a curse,
Can this day get any worse?

Thomas McAloon (10)
Delves Lane Junior School, Consett

Disaster

There was an earthquake heading to town
And made a huge building fall down.
People were terrified and a lot a people died
People still drive screaming, police car beaming.
Children getting swept away, it will be the end of the day.
At the end of the quake, I could only see a lake.

Kieron Johnson (10)
Delves Lane Junior School, Consett

Disaster!

Tsunamis - life risking.
Higher than any wave.
No one can withstand it,
No one can be brave!

Playing at the beach.
Having fun with my bucket and spade
My face is in shock
Here comes a tidal wave!

Tsunamis always take down everything in their path!

Conor Metcalfe (10)
Delves Lane Junior School, Consett

Miss Gillie

You're Mr Lonley blasting in the sky.
You're as tasty as chips and chicken nuggets.
You're as ruby-red as a sunset.
You're as smooth as a strawberry smoothie slipping down my throat.
A black and white panda sitting on the long grass.
You're as hot as Ibiza.
You're as sunny as a summer's day.

Leona Wilson (7)
Delves Lane Junior School, Consett

Jill

You're like a pop party singer,
You're like a juicy Sunday dinner,
You're like a silky blue,
You're like a tangerine Fanta,
You're like my cherry-red tracksuit bottoms,
You're like a sunset in Cyprus,
You're like a happy face in my life.

Anna Eland (8)
Delves Lane Junior School, Consett

Disaster

I heard a big bang one day
I knew I had to run away
I was getting really scared
Then people crying I heard
There was a volcano destroying the town
Buildings were falling down
It was the end of life for everyone and anyone.

Courtney Clark (10)
Delves Lane Junior School, Consett

Disaster!

Deadly and dangerous tornadoes
Coming towards me
Dark and dull skies
Dust is in my eyes
I can't see a thing
It's still coming towards me, I can feel it
Things are flying everywhere
If I run it won't make any difference
It will still get me.

Kyle Routledge (10)
Delves Lane Junior School, Consett

Tsunami

I watched as the big wave came closer and closer.
I was beginning to panic.
Everyone on the beach was screaming.
Unexpectedly the tsunami came crashing down
And wrecked my city.
I watched in horror, my city was destroyed.

Kate McGuigan (10)
Delves Lane Junior School, Consett

Disaster

Earthquake, earthquake, run away
Earthquake, earthquake, I hate today
Earthquake, earthquake, wrecked my house
Earthquake, earthquake, killed my mouse
Earthquake, earthquake, don't get me
Earthquake, earthquake, wreck that tree.

Connor Robinson (9)
Delves Lane Junior School, Consett

Disaster Tornadoes

Dark, gloomy sky
Terrible hundred mile an hour winds
The violent clashing of buildings
Horrified people running for their lives
Blast of lightning frying everything in its path
Aggressive winds reaching three hundred miles an hour
Dead corpses scattered all over town.

Lauren East (10)
Delves Lane Junior School, Consett

Disaster

One day I was at school
When an earthquake struck again
The tables were shaking
The place was sizzling
Like a frying pan
It's time for death
The place was a tip
Houses were breaking in half
We had nowhere to go!

Autumn Colgrave (9)
Delves Lane Junior School, Consett

Disaster

Waves crashing into rocks
People dying under the water
Rumbling the ground
Buildings panicked
The whole town screaming
Roads collapsing
Babies crying
Children dying
Adults lying
Everyone dead!

Deanna Elliott (9)
Delves Lane Junior School, Consett

Disaster

Tornadoes, destructive storm,
Called the clashing death
Powerful, deadly streak of wind
Running through the city
Dramatic nuclear storm
A powerful, deadly disaster
People scared
Tornado gets closer
This is it - time for death.

Bethany Smith (10)
Delves Lane Junior School, Consett

Earthquakes

Mum and I were out at the shops
And all of a sudden the road went *pop!*
It was an earthquake, people were running for their lives,
Their family could not believe their *eyes!*
They had never seen anything like it,
Many houses and shops being destroyed,
It was truly *shocking!*

Frances Boyle (10)
Delves Lane Junior School, Consett

Stephanie

You're like the sound of pop music going through my ear
You're like some eggs, beans and cheese on toast on a cold day
You're as yellow as the shining sun
You're like a glass of lemonade on a hot day
You're like a fish eating its food
You're like the marvellous Metro Centre
You make me as happy as can be.

Chloe Bell (8)
Delves Lane Junior School, Consett

Grandma

You're like Hilary Duff singing great
You're like a juicy pasta on a cold day
You're like a silk red wool
You're like a fizzy Coke on a hot day
You're like some tracksuits from JJB Sports
You're like a sunset from Sharm el Shiek
You're like the happy days from my life.

Georgia Bowman (9)
Delves Lane Junior School, Consett

Mrs Short

You're Kylie blasting loud in my bedroom
You're a gorgeous piece of chocolate cake
You're a beautiful drink of Pepsi
You're a sunny day at a place in Spain
You're a resting day on Sunday.

Charlotte Colgrave (7)
Delves Lane Junior School, Consett

My Brother

You're like a Green Day song blasting in my head
You're like a juicy chicken
You're like the midnight sky twinkling
A bubbling lemonade can, fizzing in my hands
You're like a witch's cat
You're like a trip to York
And winning a really long race.

Bryce Freeman (9)
Delves Lane Junior School, Consett

Mam

You're like a red rose
You're like a crispy turkey twizzler
You're like a light shade of blue
I always like cuddles off you
You are the best person in my life
You're like Ronan Keating singing live
You're like a cup of fizzy lemonade
You always make me feel happy
I like spending Fridays with you.

Abbie Ross (7)
Delves Lane Junior School, Consett

My Mammy

You're like the disco playing Girls Aloud 'Love Machine'
You're like the tastiest jam tart I have ever eaten
You're like the loveliest purple in the rainbow
You're like my lovely warm jumper
You're like my bedroom you made me
You're like the lovely taste of orange juice
Slowly running down my throat
You're like my joyful face when I am waking up.

Jemma Whaley (7)
Delves Lane Junior School, Consett

Rebecca

You're like Girls Aloud blasting in my bedroom
You're like a tasty McDonald's
You're as red as a ruby
You're like a bubbling can
You're like a cowgirl running through the forest
You're like a splash in Wet 'n' Wild
You make me happy every day
You're like a summer breeze in July
You're like a dog barking in the night.

Louise Brown (7)
Delves Lane Junior School, Consett

Dog In The Basket

Dog in the basket, what do you hear?
I hear . . .
The naughty children fighting
The big TV singing
The rusty washing machine spinning
The smelly oven clanging
I hear . . .
The stupid cat eating
The little cupboard swinging
The vicious hamster nibbling
The shiny fridge buzzing
That's what I hear.

Dana Dixon (9)
Delves Lane Junior School, Consett

Courtney

You're like a famous pop star
You're like a creamy toffee cake
You're like a lilac flower in the summer
You're like the creamiest milk I have ever tasted
You're a fuming lion with big sharp teeth
You're a happy person
You're a magical time in Disneyland
You're a happy person
You are like the best summer
You are a lovely Monday dinner.

Alyce Carter (8)
Delves Lane Junior School, Consett

Joanne

You're 'American Idiot' by Green Day on my MP3 player
You're old lasagne, a bit chewy but still edible
You're as gold as the eclipse moving out of the way of the sun
You're as lovely as a Carlsberg lager
You're as nice as sightseeing in Spain
You're like my jagged jeans scraping
When I sit next to you I feel loved.

Matthew Lamb (9)
Delves Lane Junior School, Consett

Dylan

You're a Green Day song blasting out of a CD player.
You're a nice Pepsi drink in a can.
You're a delicious pepperoni pizza.
You're a blue summer's day in the sky.
Your feeling is like crocodile skin.
Every time I'm with you I'm at Blackpool.
When I'm next to you, you're as fast as a cheetah.

Ethan Waller (8)
Delves Lane Junior School, Consett

Volcano

There was a volcano about to explode,
All of the debris shot out on the road,
All of the lava the volcano spat out,
You will get killed there is no doubt!

All of the lava gushing out of the vent,
Watch out, it might spill over your tent,
All of the lava up in the air,
Watch out and take more care!

Thomas Ryan (10)
Delves Lane Junior School, Consett

Volcanoes

Millions of volcanoes in the world
Behold the fear they let out
People that run wild screaming
Shouting, climbing out
Frowning
Covered in brown ash
Nervous when it blew
Scared as it started to spew.

Dylan Elsdon (9)
Delves Lane Junior School, Consett

Tsunami

T is for terrified
S is for shaking
U is for unbelievable
N is for nature dying
A is for afraid
M is for monstrous
I is for inner soul.

Nico Jeffrey (10)
Delves Lane Junior School, Consett

Earthquakes

E is for earthquakes, crashing things
A is for agony
R is for rumbling, when I feel scared
T is for terrified, standing there watching everything
H is for horrible, seeing people die
Q is for Queen, hearing the kids screaming for their mum
U is for utter shock
A is for animals shaking in their cages
K is for kids sadly dying
E is for extremely dangerous
S is for sad mums crying for their children.

Chantelle Bessford (10)
Delves Lane Junior School, Consett

Volcanoes

There was lava shooting on the road,
People screaming in front of me,
Dying with sadness,
Children running for their mam and dad,
Helicopters flying over saving people,
News cameras watching.

Kieran Whitwood (10)
Delves Lane Junior School, Consett

Volcanoes

Lava flowing, people grabbing children.
Screaming, while they run for their lives,
The lava running like a vicious dog running to get you,
While it melts your bones,
Lava splashing in the air hitting people in the eyes,
Gushing blood splashing in the air,
Bones turning into toothpicks,
Brains turning into mush.

Connor Balmer (10)
Delves Lane Junior School, Consett

Disasters

A deadly tornado is smashing down schools
Sucking up builders' raggy old tools
Destroying all the people, extremely lethal
Someone looked out in the night
It sure gave them a fright
In the street was death
I could see a neighbour called Jeff,
There was no gladness
There was just madness.

Jordan Gibson (10)
Delves Lane Junior School, Consett

Ashley

You're like a lonely singer singing quietly
You're like a roast chicken dinner on Sunday
You're as red as a morning sunrise
You're the Coca-Cola running down my throat
You're as soft as my Rooney top
You're the hottest holiday I've been on
You are as beautiful as a green island.

Daniel Farthing (8)
Delves Lane Junior School, Consett

The Golden Beach

Upon the beach of Tenerife
Sea creatures swimming
In cold, sparkling seas
Whilst crabs walk on the golden sand
Nipping people's feet
Glaring seagulls eating golden breadcrumbs
Cliff faces, falling down, crumbling stone.

Ashley Parkin (11)
Easington Colliery Primary School, Peterlee

Blackpool

Blackpool beach
Sea goes flowing
Teachers try to teach
About this tiny thing growing.

The shows go flying
All day long
The parents always keep trying
To play a little game of ping-pong.

Candyfloss slides down your throat
Careful though, don't choke
Children always wear a coat
To block away their parent's smoke.

Hannah Cook (11)
Easington Colliery Primary School, Peterlee

Tavistock

Underneath rock and grass,
Where there used to be loads of gas.
A town where there used to be raids,
Where loads of people got paid.

There is a little town called Tavistock,
Where there is a massive clock.
There is a special person called Sir Francis Drake,
He lived by a little lake.

There's a legend called the Hairy Hand,
He got killed by a frying pan!
Take a trip up to the moor,
Which is Devon's core.

Scott Wardle (10)
Easington Colliery Primary School, Peterlee

Paphos

Paphos, a great place to be
Come and see the sun and sea.
Lauren - my super niece
Give me some peace
On my super holiday
My two big sisters
Coming with me
To Paphos, a great place to be!

Sean Fish (11)
Easington Colliery Primary School, Peterlee

Sunny Holidays

H appy holidays they are so much fun
O nly problem they cost too much
L ove is all around on holiday
I t is so horrible if you get sunburnt
D ads and mums are so protective
A ll the sunscreen getting slapped on
Y ou are so lucky to go on holiday
S o many people are in the swimming pool.

Sophie Carr (10)
Easington Colliery Primary School, Peterlee

Roller Coaster

Flying all over, swinging left to right
Quick, scary, fun, exciting
But you have to be a certain height
Roller coasters here, there and everywhere
Weather burning, scalding
I bet you wouldn't dare!

Meghan Robson (11)
Easington Colliery Primary School, Peterlee

Alicante

Walking along the rough sandy pavement
To the smooth rippled pools.
Dropping spectacular Euros
Diving, bombing, swimming
Front stroke, back stroke,
Butterfly, you know the stuff.
Cheap drinks in glamorous pubs
In the corner an old, dusty pool table
Don't touch, it will collapse.

At the end of a lovely day
Look up in the sky
And there you will find
The only star.

Arron Musgrove (11)
Easington Colliery Primary School, Peterlee

Cyprus

Beaches in Cyprus are like golden breadcrumbs
Seagulls like air horns
The hot temperature like a boiler
Hotels big as skyscrapers
Ice creams like frozen diamonds
Cliffs like tombstones
Roads smooth like German roads
A clear sea like a window.

James Johnson (10)
Easington Colliery Primary School, Peterlee

Villa

You will live the life of luxury in a villa
It'll be a side killer
Live the life with a cellar
You never know you might meet a fella.

Take a walk to the pool
People will think you're pretty cool
If you're sick of taking a dip
Why don't you try a flip.

If you sneeze
Just breathe in the breeze
Not the dust
Although you might not be fussed.

Carl Price (11)
Easington Colliery Primary School, Peterlee

Go On A Holiday

Go on a holiday, you know you want to
See different fish, colours galore
Go on an adventure and see all the wildlife
Go to Alcudia, you know you want to
And you'll want to stay there for your life.

Go on a water slide, jump over waves
Go down little slides, go down big
Go to Alcudia, you know you want to
And you'll want to stay there for your life.

Go to the beach, you could go snorkelling, diving as well
See the golden sand, build sandcastles
Go to Alcudia, you know you want to
And you'll want to stay there for your life.

So what do you think?
Of all the things you can do
But there's still plenty more in store for you
So go! Go! Go!

Amy-Leigh McAndrew (11)
Easington Colliery Primary School, Peterlee

Holidays

Holidays, holidays everywhere, take a plane or even a train
Take a pan and don't forget your old nan
Sun, sea, sand, waiting for you and see the big brass band
Eagle chasing the rabbit and the seagull
Diving into the sparkling sea to get his tea.

Natalie Carr (11)
Easington Colliery Primary School, Peterlee

Off To Spain

Off to Spain, out of the rain, have stuff to do
On the beach, in the water, loads of people, too.

Dogs and kids in the sea, swimming ever so far
Swimming out so far, further than a car.

Fish and sharks in the sea, everybody's scared
All the kids are running home and paired.

Steven Pearce (11)
Easington Colliery Primary School, Peterlee

Crete

C ollecting shells by the sea
R unning along the seashore
E nding the day with a meal
T rampling on the rock pools
E nd, what a shame.

Shannon Stobbs (10)
Easington Colliery Primary School, Peterlee

Beach

The sound of the beach, the rocky seashore
Who could ask for more than the sun and shore?
Waves splash around, look what I've just found
The beach is cool like a game of pool
The rocks are sharp, argh! Look there's a shark
The sun is going down, now it's time to say goodbye
The shore will call again.

Alice Marshall (10)
Easington Colliery Primary School, Peterlee

At The Beach

I'll soon be at the beach, with a pool full of leeches
It is too deep to reach, the pool full of leeches.

I will settle down here and get a cold beer
The sea is very near, but I'd rather chill here.

I'll lay down on my mat and take off my hat
And there, a sneaky cat with a burger full of fat
I'll just lay down on my mat.

I eat a hammy bun and the sea is full of fun
Until I finish my hammy bun, now there is no fun.

It is starting to get dark, all through the park,
I will have to eat the last of my lime, so I can get home on time.

Robert Longstaff (11)
Easington Colliery Primary School, Peterlee

The Beach

The day at the beach, tasting the peach
The golden sand, running through my hand
The wind blowing through my hair
I love the beach, although I care
Watching the fish swim by
Seagulls in the corner of my eye.

Seaweed floating on the waters
Seeing a man with his daughters
It makes me think of my family
And all my old memories.

Chariti Boland (11)
Easington Colliery Primary School, Peterlee

Portugal

In the pool lovely and warm, lots of friends playing ball
Got to get a tan before we go home
Very silly Nan, all wrapped up in a winter coat.

Fresh fish smelling out the nearby town
Sand in my toes, lush and soft
Sea air among fishing boats,
Very silly Nan, all slopped in suntan lotion.

In the airport, sad and glum, got to go home, snug and warm
On the aeroplane, close my eyes
When I open them, Nan's a surprise
She's in her swimming costume!

Samantha Emerson (10)
Easington Colliery Primary School, Peterlee

The Museum At Seaham

I went to a museum in Seaham
I met a boy called Ray and a girl called Faye
There was an old yeti it was eating spaghetti
A person took us on a tour
The guide was extremely poor
There was a tank and a caveman called Frank
We went to the gift shop
My mam bought an old-fashioned clock
Faye bought a bone, Ray bought a phone
That was my visit to Seaham!

Daniel Williamson (11)
Easington Colliery Primary School, Peterlee

Country Blues

G reece is very cheap, everywhere there's markets
R estaurant's food very good, you could eat it every day
E very place is very hot, you would wish you could stay for as long
                                                        as you want

E very sea as clear as glass
C lear water, see the lovely fish
E very beach is burning your feet walking on the shoreside.

Jordan Robinson (11)
Easington Colliery Primary School, Peterlee

Maspalomas

M aspalomas is great
A nd with all the sand and sea
S omeone hurt their knee
P utting at minigolf
A fter a long day's swimming
L ong paths to the pool
O n the hundredth floor
M emories of Maspalomas
A s we fly away
S ometimes I write to my mate.

James Dunn (10)
Easington Colliery Primary School, Peterlee

Florida

F antastic Florida

L anding at Orlando airport

O rlando, the home of Walt Disney

R iding on a roller coaster faster than anyone else

I nteresting things to do every day

D isneyland is full of fun and adventure

A t the sunny beach all day long.

Sarah Bainbridge (10)
Easington Colliery Primary School, Peterlee

Salou

S eeing the beautiful sand
A sking to go to the beach
L oving the beautiful land
O nly me wanting to go
U sing my sunglasses to look up high.

Courtney Hornsby (11)
Easington Colliery Primary School, Peterlee

Cyprus

C yprus has lots of things for you
Y ou can go swimming and there's lots you want to do
P ull your bikini on and jump right in
R ather be here than at home putting trash in the bin
U sually there are chips you can buy at the store
S upernoodles and plenty more.

Lauren Stockdale (11)
Easington Colliery Primary School, Peterlee

Blackpool

Blackpool is my favourite place
That's why I have a large suitcase
The tower is as tall as a tree
And I also like the shiny sea.

I ran up the tower as fast as I could
Right to the top and then I stopped and stood
There in front of me was a clown
But all I did was stand and frown.

The rides were near the beach
All of a sudden something ran across the deck, it was a leech
Then we went to dine
But the restaurant was blocked by a line.

We had popcorn and toffee apples
And we visited some old chapels
It was nearly time to go home
But when we went I left my bright blue comb.

Rebecca Jones (11)
Easington Colliery Primary School, Peterlee

Beach

B eaches are wonderful places to visit
E xciting things to do and play
A s the children play in the cool refreshing sea
C rispy golden sand crunching as you walk on it
H ow beautiful the beaches are.

Kyle Anderson (11)
Easington Colliery Primary School, Peterlee

Blackpool

B lackpool has a big tower
L ots of bright and beautiful flowers
A ll around the shops you see
C an you see my aunt Dee?
K ites in the air, sailing high
P ool in the bar, playing I-spy
O n the plane it was so far to travel
O n the sunny beach all day
L ovely times I don't want to forget.

Jennifer Creed (10)
Easington Colliery Primary School, Peterlee

France

F rance is a lovely place to dance with a ballroom full of plants
R un to the Eiffel Tower, run with might and power
A nd there I bought some pants with little green ants
N ot knowing where to go, I sat and watched the show
C ould just say I found my way down the tower, I ran like a flower
E ventually I went home, the tall tower became small,
    as I slowly drove out of sight, then it became dark as I needed a
    shiny night light.

Kieran Charlton (11)
Easington Colliery Primary School, Peterlee

Beach

One day I went to the beach
While I was there I had a lovely juicy peach
The sand was crunching like a crisp
And there was a lady there who had a lisp.

All the fish were swishing
While we were fishing
We were licking lollies all day
Well, until the birds took them away.

Stephanie Kendall (10)
Easington Colliery Primary School, Peterlee

I'm Going To Turkey

I'm going to Turkey to enjoy a holiday
I can't wait to go there to find the magic key
My heart was beating so fast when my dad got his pay
This holiday will be cool, cool as can be
Sorry, haven't got time to chat we're going to set off
Stop staring at me you dancing tree
My stomach is rumbling with a strange feeling
Flying through the sky with bubbles as clouds
My baby brother is quietly squealing
When we get there we will have to change my money into pounds.

Lauren Murray (10)
Easington Colliery Primary School, Peterlee

Paris

P aris in the summer is a beautiful sight
A rc d'Triumph a magnificent landmark
R ising from the centre is the Eiffel Tower
I n Paris is a big blue, magnificent skyline
S eine, that flows through the heart of Paris.

Jonathan Humphries (11)
Easington Colliery Primary School, Peterlee

Eaden Camp

E aden Camp is just the best
A nd it's even better than the rest
D o you like it or have you been?
E veryone thinks it's the best sight you've ever seen
N obody thinks the bunks are very comfortable

C artons emptied on an outside table
A nyone would think it's the best place to be
M ostly because it's World War II, you'll see
P lay at the old park all day it's a great place to play.

Katie Randall (10)
Easington Colliery Primary School, Peterlee

Car

I bought a car, navy blue
It came with a spoiler too
Turbo engine, diesel through
That will make me really cool
Leather seats, turbo power
It will make me go 200mph
Blinging wheels full of chrome
That will make me go to the throne.

Andrew Duff (11)
Easington Colliery Primary School, Peterlee

My Car

I bought a car, navy blue
Alloy wheels, a spoiler too.
Turbo-charged diesel fuel
That will make me really cool
Blitzing through the streets
With *boom, boom* beats
Metallic finish and bodywork
That will make it just like Kirk
My car is flash
And I can sell it for a lot of cash
If it stalls
I'll go berserk
Anyway I'm busy today
I'm selling it on eBay.

John-Paul Purcell (11)
Easington Colliery Primary School, Peterlee

My Dog Murphy

M urphy the miniature Schnauzer
Y ou would love him, he is so cute

D ad doesn't agree
O nly Murphy swims in the sea
G ood boy with great growl

M agnificent runner, take your
U mbrella
R aining or not he'll
P ull you outside
H ow much I love him
Y ou'll never know.

Ellie Robson (10)
Easington Colliery Primary School, Peterlee

The Beach

Beautiful views are found at the beach
Everyone hears the dolphins screech
And every day the tide goes *swish, swish.*
Collect the shells and make a wish
Remember to take your bucket and spade
And play with all the friends you have made.

Bethany Knight (10)
Easington Colliery Primary School, Peterlee

Newcastle United

N UFC
E verywhere in Newcastle
W hite and black shirts
C oming to the match
A way from home
S hearer and Owen
T ime - full time and half-time
L oving the team
E veryone celebrating, we've just won!

U nited forever
N ice weather
I n the back of the net
T oon Army
E mre Bebzoglu, Shay Given and Steve Harper
D own in the stadium.

Sophie Houghton (10)
Easington Colliery Primary School, Peterlee

Skiing At Silksworth

S ilksworth we shall start off at

K eep yourself warm - wear a woolly hat

I n case you bang your head on the rough mat

I taly we will travel to next

N ight-time comes, who is the best?

G etting ready for the day ahead

T oday is the day we learn to jump

R ide around, jump over the bump!

I nside we shall eat our dinner

P ila is the place to be if you're a beginner!

Kirsty Kell (11)
Easington Colliery Primary School, Peterlee

At The Zoo

I went to a zoo last week,
I saw a pelican with a long beak.
When I ran around the corner I saw a flamingo,
And when I looked again it was playing bingo.
Then I looked in a cage and there was a gorilla,
It was asleep on a big fluffy pillow.
In the reptile house I saw a snake,
It never saw me because it was too busy eating a cake.
Later that day as a treat,
I got to walk near a crocodile's feet.
The lion in the cage started to roar,
So I offered him some crisps and he gave me his paw.
I hope you enjoyed your trip to the zoo,
I'll have to go now because I need the loo.

Joe Foster (11)
Easington Colliery Primary School, Peterlee

My Dad Thinks He's Elvis

My dad thinks he's Elvis,
When he swings his pelvis.
It's a spectacular show to see,
We get free tickets, Mum and me.
Girls enter a trance,
When he starts to dance.
When he tries to croon,
All old women swoon.

I wish he were a normal dad,
But on the whole, he's not that bad!

Marley Rollins (10)
Easington Colliery Primary School, Peterlee

The Car

I bought a car, navy blue
It had a spoiler and alloys too.
Turbo engine, diesel fuel
That will make me really cool.
Leather seats, turbo power
It makes me go 100mph.
Roof scoop is the best
Makes my car better than the rest.
Really big wheels, fit for a truck
Got them from Michelin what a stroke of luck.
Fancy details all the rest
Let my friends take it out for a test.
My car is cool, my car is class
I could sell it for a lot of cash.

Ryan Wade (11)
Easington Colliery Primary School, Peterlee

SAFC

Stadium of Light is the name of the ground,
But no wins of matches have ever been found.

We went up the steps, 1, 2, 3, 4,
Are we doing well now? The answer is no.

We defended, we dribbled, eventually scored,
I take it the Sunderland fans were bored.

The medals, the trophy, oh some noise,
We scored because we had the right boys.

We are not doing well I say with a frown,
I'll have to go with Sunderland, down, down and down.

Jordan Scott (10)
Easington Colliery Primary School, Peterlee

Football

F ootballs were falling as fast as a flash
O n people's heads they were going dash, dash, dash
O pen the door and I saw people hitting footballs at my door
T elevisions blasting more, more, more
B alls hitting people in the face
A ll the people shouting, 'What a disgrace.'
L ines on the football were very blue
L ightning striking, lots of people start getting spots.

Michael Bryce (10)
Easington Colliery Primary School, Peterlee

Seasons All Around

Autumn fall,
Leaves so bright,
With colours that are your delight,
They fall from the trees onto the ground,
All around,
All around.

Winter arrives,
Crisp and cold,
Children playing in the snow,
Snowballs flying,
All around,
All around.

Spring is here,
Blossoming sights,
Daffodils and snowdrops alight,
Birds are singing,
All around,
All around.

Summertime
Sun shines bright,
Children playing into the night,
Happy faces,
All around,
All around.

Sarah Walker (11)
Easington Colliery Primary School, Peterlee

Nana's House

When I go down to my nana's,
It is such a treat,
She lives in London,
All tidy and neat,
As she speaks,
She sits me down,
I listen to her voice in my ear,
She is getting near,
Tears flood my face,
I do up my lace,
Ready to run,
But she is . . .
My nana has gone,
My grandad is there,
It has been so long,
I wish I could be there.

Georgia Dawson (11)
Easington Colliery Primary School, Peterlee

The Rhino

The rhino smashes a wall
It is grey and big
Its feet crash on the road
Cars are thrown into buildings.

Thomas Brown (10)
Ingleton CE Primary School, Darlington

The Tornado

A tornado spins round and round,
Just like a bull pawing at the ground,
The tornado whirls and rumbles past,
While the bull charges at full blast,
Dark and speedy, noisy and scary,
Whirling wind is temporary.

Jennifer Stephenson (10)
Ingleton CE Primary School, Darlington

The Circus

(Based on 'The Sound Collector' by Roger McGough)

'A stranger called this morning
Dressed all in black and grey
Put every sound into a bag
And carried them away'.

The roaring of the lion
The shouting of the clown
The squeaking of the gymnast
The crackling of the conductor's crown.

The silence of the tightrope walker
The doo, doo, doodling of the music
The drumming of the drummer
The cheering as the monkey does a trick.

'A stranger called this morning
He didn't leave his name
Left us all in silence,
Life will never be the same'.

Roger Dunn (9)
Ingleton CE Primary School, Darlington

The Lion

The lion is getting hungry
He is roaring and roaring
His tummy is rumbling
He has a mane of golden lightning
And fur of fluffy clouds
All grey and black in the night sky
With a big twisted tail like a tornado.

Dale Deary (9)
Ingleton CE Primary School, Darlington

The Sound Collector

(Based on 'The Sound Collector' by Roger McGough)

'A stranger called this morning
Dressed all in black and grey
Put every sound into a bag
And carried them away'.

The roaring of the lion, the hissing of a snake
And when the zebra gallops a screaming noise it makes.
The howling of the wolf, the roar of the bear
The yawning of the hippo and the shouting of the mares.

The chomping of the tiger, the stomping of the rhino
The buzzing of the bees, the scratching of the armadillo.
The snapping of the crocodile, the scratching of the fox
The laughing of the hyena climbing over the rocks.

The bubbling of the fish, the flapping of the penguins
The splashing of the flamingos, the clucking of the hens.

'A stranger called this morning
He didn't leave his name
Left us only in silence
Life will never be the same'.

Lucinda Elliott (10)
Ingleton CE Primary School, Darlington

The Sound Collector

(Based on 'The Sound Collector' by Roger McGough)

'A stranger called this morning
Dressed in black and grey
Put every sound into a bag
And carried them away'.

The shouting of the children
The bouncing of the balls
The screaming of the teachers
The crying on the floor.

The crash of the window
The shot of the ball
The scream of the girl
As she's going to fall.

'A stranger called this morning
He didn't leave his name
Left us only silence
Life will never be the same'.

William Forster (9)
Ingleton CE Primary School, Darlington

The Sound Collector

(Based on 'The Sound Collector' by Roger McGough)

A stranger called at dinner time
Dressed in black and grey
Put every sound into a bag
And carried them away.

The shouting of the children
The creaking of the chairs
The whiff of the garlic bread
The pulling of the hairs.

The squeaking of the floor
As we start to run
The talking of the cook
As we were having fun.

The ticking of the hour
The hissing of the heater
Dinner can't be over
Here comes the teacher.

The crying of the children
As they've been hit
Tired dinner nannies
Oh no, someone's been bit.

A stranger called at dinner time
He didn't leave his name
Left us only silence
Life will never be the same.

Charlotte Payne (9)
Ingleton CE Primary School, Darlington

The End Of The School Day

The children boiling, bubbling ready to explode
Like a volcano ready to erupt.

When they hear the bell ring
They pop and explode and gush out of the door,
Bashing everything in their path.

Jumping, rumbling with joy
Parents hiding from the children with fear in their eyes
People screaming and shouting, 'Help, it's home time.'

Sally Robinson (9)
Ingleton CE Primary School, Darlington

The Polar Bear

The polar bear runs around like a blizzard of snow
With danger in his eyes and a cold, wet nose
With his claws he nips your face
When he sleeps, he is very still
His fur blankets the ground
Then his teeth will shimmer
A winter wonderland of snow
You will see a polar bear dashing around with glee.

Libby Duffy (9)
Ingleton CE Primary School, Darlington

The Jumblies

In a sieve they went to sea, they did
In a sieve they went to sea.
A squid attacked them very fast
First the sieve and then the mast.
While they were at sea
This is the end of our good life
But the Jumblies found a carving knife
They stabbed the squid in the back
Soon the water all went black
While they were at sea
Far and few, far and few
Are the lands where the Jumblies live
Their heads are green and their hands are blue
And they went to sea in a sieve.

Becky Duffy (11)
Ingleton CE Primary School, Darlington

The Disco Poem

Everybody gushes through the doors,
Everybody sizzling with excitement
People rocking to the beat,
People getting all sweaty and hot,
Everybody getting bubbly drinks,
Everybody exploding to the floor,
People destroying every balloon,
People shouting, 'Boom, boom, boom!'

Rebecca Toms (10)
Ingleton CE Primary School, Darlington

Schoolchildren

Engines starting, ready to go,
Leaving the classroom as the bell rings,
Changing gears, catching up with friends,
Traffic light teachers stop you in your path
Slamming on the nitro as you leave the school
Home
Final stop.

Connor Redgrave (11)
Ingleton CE Primary School, Darlington

The Tornado

The tornado is like a digger
Moving houses and cars out of its way
Digging up everything and anyone in its path.

A tornado is like an angry person
Throwing objects away,
Throwing here and there
Like a footballer taking a throw-in.

A tornado is like a Hoover
Sucking up junk and dumping it in the bin
Along with last year's lot.

A tornado is like Taz
Spinning around to move from house to house
Chewing on houses like bones.

Then the tornado goes to sleep
And waits for the next storm to start
And wrecks all the homes and harms people.

But when will the tornado learn
To get along with mankind?

Matthew Simpson (11)
Ingleton CE Primary School, Darlington

At A Footie Match

Fans gush into the stadium
Rumbling through the turnstile
Boiling up to the seats
Sizzling to get started
Smoky because they've gone and scored
Gone red, they missed a penalty
Flow down at half-time
Hot and ready for the second half
Bubbling, singing their chant
Booming to get something to eat.

Phillip Dennis (9)
Ingleton CE Primary School, Darlington

The Sound Collector

(Based on 'The Sound Collector' by Roger McGough)

'A stranger called this morning
Dressed all in black and grey
Put every sound into a bag
And carried them away'.

The rattling of the tractor
The barking of the dogs
The neighing of the horses
When they jump the logs.

The mooing of the cows
The cracking when eggs drop
The honking of the sow
The rustling of the crop.

'A stranger called this morning
He didn't leave his name
Left us only silence
Life will never be the same'.

Edmund Clarke (10)
Ingleton CE Primary School, Darlington

The Sound Collector

(Based on 'The Sound Collector' by Roger McGough)

'A stranger called this morning
Dressed all in black and grey
Put every sound into a bag
And carried them away'.

The cheering of the fans
The revving of the cars
The banging of the footballs
The squeaking of the bars.

The shouting of the visitors
The chattering of the men
When you see the players
The screaming of my friend Ben.

The hissing of the enemies
The clapping of the people
The beeping of the cars
The dripping of the treacle.

'A stranger called this morning
He didn't leave his name
Left us only silence
Life will never be the same'.

Christopher Parker (10)
Ingleton CE Primary School, Darlington

The Football Match

(Based on 'The Sound Collector' by Roger McGough)

'A stranger called this morning
Dressed all in black and grey
Put every sound into a bag
And carried them away'.

The boo of the crowd
The bang of the football
The roaring at the football match
The shouting from the stall.

The referee's final whistle
The banging on the plastic
The sizzle of the beef
The snapping of the elastic.

'A stranger called this morning
He didn't leave his name
He left us only silence
Life will never be the same'.

Peter Forster (9)
Ingleton CE Primary School, Darlington

One Colourful Dream

I woke up one day . . .
And went berserk at my mam
For dying my clothes and my bedroom
Pink, purple and girly colours!
My friend was coming
And I couldn't let him see my pink clothes
Or my house for that matter
Then in my head I heard an echo
Saying, 'Aunty Betty's here.'
Then I felt a hand on my shoulder
And I closed my eyes
After a while I opened them
Finally I woke up on the floor,
'Jason, it's 2pm get up,' Mam said.

Jason Maguire (9)
Raventhorpe Preparatory School, Darlington

When I Woke Up

When I woke up I was floating in the air,
When I woke up I didn't give a care,
When I woke up the whole house was blue,
When I woke up my dog had the flu,
When I woke up the fridge was upside down,
When I woke up I gave a great big frown,
When I woke up the sky was green,
When I woke up I couldn't believe what I'd seen,
When I woke up the walls were made of jelly,
When I woke up I had a rumbly belly,
When I woke up the lights were flickering,
When I woke up my sister was bickering,
Enough of this, I don't want to wake up,
I'm going to start counting sheep to get back to sleep.

Imogen Storey (10)
Raventhorpe Preparatory School, Darlington

Sweets

S is for sweets - there are lots of different kinds.
W is for Wonka bars - so melty and delicious.
E is for everlasting gobstoppers that are sweet and juicy.
E is for endless chewing gum that is so chewy.
T is for ten packets of cola bottles.
S is for sherbet - so sour and fizzy.

Laura Marriott (9)
Raventhorpe Preparatory School, Darlington

A Cat And Twelve Fish

When I'm at home
I have twelve fish.
The problem is I have a cat
And when I'm not looking
It jumps up high
And scares the fish -
Sometimes they die.

Charlotte Whittaker (10)
Raventhorpe Preparatory School, Darlington

The Land Of Treats

I saw an old woman,
She gave me a seed
And said it would turn into a big tall weed.
I did according to all she said,
In a huge flower bed.
Make a wish, do not balk,
Then,
Go,
Climb up the stalk.
So up I climbed
And saw the land of treats.
I hope there will be lots of sweets!
I wandered around and found what I wanted,
Then down I went, down the weed again -
The weed that sprouted
From a tiny little seed.

Naomi Duncan (10)
Raventhorpe Preparatory School, Darlington

Animals

There are lots of animals,
Different shapes and sizes.
Some are small, tall, big or fat,
Some have four legs, some two.
Some have one, sometimes none.
They are different colours -
Black, white, green, yellow, brown and grey.
I like them all but most of all, my dog.

Saffron Pickup (9)
Raventhorpe Preparatory School, Darlington

Santa's Elves

Nobody knows
How much they think of ideas
Of what to make for presents
For you and me.
They work all year around
The world.
You close your eyes and sleep -
Wake up and there's a treat.
Reindeer fly back
And there's a repeat -
Ready for next year.

William Richardson (9)
Raventhorpe Preparatory School, Darlington

Autumn

I love autumn,
The brown, red, gold and hazel coloured leaves,
The sharp cold air,
The breeze in the trees
And the bonfires which flare.

Autumn is good for Hallowe'en and spooks
And ghostly tales in ghostly books,
Autumn is good,
I love autumn.

Tom Knox (9)
Raventhorpe Preparatory School, Darlington

Holidays

I've been on loads of holidays
And this is most of them
I met a man in Milan
Lost a sneaker in Costa Rica
I was ill in Brazil
Pulled my Achilles in Chile
I went to the loo in Peru
Did a dance in France
Got some ale in Wales
Went insane in Spain
Got caught by the police in Nice
I felt finer in China
Put on weight in Kuwait
What did I do in Tibet?
I forget
And went home!

Andrew Smith (10)
Raventhorpe Preparatory School, Darlington

Friends Are Cool

F is for Frankie, my cousin and mate
R is for Robert who is never late
I is for Imogen I see every day
E is for Emily, saw her at the bay
N is for Nicole, she left last year
D is for Darius he never sheds a tear
S is for Sarah, she's really cool

A is for Alex he always wears a top
R is for Ryan who plays with guns, *pop!*
E is for Elly who I saw with Kelly

C is for Chelsey, that's little old me
O is for Olivia, she is really funny
O is for Oliver, he left last year too
L is for Louise and Leah, my two identical cousins,
very annoying too.
Friends are really cool.

Chelsey Peart (10)
Raventhorpe Preparatory School, Darlington

Snowboarding

Snowboarding is really cool,
But when you fall over you feel like a fool.
Pick yourself up, dust yourself down,
Try to avoid the tears and the frown.
Start again, ignore the pain,
Snowboarding is really cool
The slopes you'll soon rule!

Grace Wray (10)
Raventhorpe Preparatory School, Darlington

The Playground Poem

Children in the playground
Running up and down
Smiling, happy faces
Never a frown.

Shouting, skipping, hopping
Going here and there
Running, jumping, leaping
High into the air.

Children in the playground
Playing all their games
Catching up with all the news
The new starters' names.

Teacher rings the bell
Time to say farewell
They don't hang heads
They don't feel sad
Because there are
Playtimes ahead.

Judith Langridge (10)
St Joseph's RC Primary School, Durham

United Colours

The colour of warmth,
The colour of roses,
The colour you won't forget.
The colour of power,
The colour of blood,
The colour you might regret!

The colour of clouds,
The colour of lilies,
The colour that's blank and bare.
The colour of snow,
The colour of teeth,
The colour that brides like to wear.

The colour of sky,
Of lavender too,
The colour when you're upset.
The colour of cold,
The colour of sea,
Have you guessed what the colours make yet?

Sarah Edwards (10)
St Joseph's RC Primary School, Durham

My Best Friend

My best friend is always there for me
And she always cares for me.

Whatever I do wrong
We can always sing a lovely song.

But the best thing about my friend
Is that we're always together
And nothing can break us apart.

Lucy Phillips (8)
St Mary's Primary School, Consett

My World

My world is big and round,
It's got lots of ground.
It's always turning around,
But it's my world and I love it!
It's perfect the way it is,
It's filled with fizzy things
From top to bottom
But sometimes it's quite rotten
But it's my world and I love it!

Sally O'Keeffe (9)
St Mary's Primary School, Consett

The Moon

The moon is like a banana,
I like to call it Hallorner,
It's like a smile of a face,
As it sits in open space.

The moon is like
A huge white balloon,
I like to listen
To its tunes.

Abbey Thompson (8)
St Mary's Primary School, Consett

Frogs

Frogs are cool from my point of view,
They're green, red, blue and many colours too,
Frogs can swim and hop
And can live under flowers.

Frogs come out at night
And in the bright of the day
They come out to play.

I would love to have a frog as my pet,
I would feed and play with my frog,
If my parents would let me . . . !

Jonathan Gorman (8)
St Mary's Primary School, Consett

The Moon

The moon is like a massive light
Shining in my face.
I wonder if it's lonely up there
Up in that dark space.

The moon is like a shining ball,
Glittering in the night.
But when I wake I'm not lonely
Because I've got that old moon's light.

The moon is white, cream and grey
Shining in massive May.
The moon has a big huge smile
It's giving lots of light to all.

Jasmine Urwin-Collier (9)
St Mary's Primary School, Consett

Winter

Ice is like water,
Ice is like glass,
Ice is like mirrors,
Hiding the dark green grass.

Snow is like diamonds,
Snow is like lace,
Snow is like feathers,
Touching my cold face.

The moon in winter,
It's like a patterned plate,
Waiting up so high,
So high in the sky.

Hope Anderson (8)
St Mary's Primary School, Consett

Newcastle Legends

Alan Shearer plays the game,
Jack Milburn played the same.
202 the record's been broke
Jackie will be remembered as a brilliant bloke
St James' Park is the pride of the town
A brilliant team, we'll never go down.

James Donnelly (9)
St Mary's Primary School, Consett

The Sun

The sun is a golden light bulb
Burning like a giant bright light.
As the sun sets the sky goes a rosy-red
Then slips into darkness.

Beth Palmer (9)
St Mary's Primary School, Consett

The Moon

The moon is like a pair of lips
Trying to find a mouth-shaped banana.

The moon is like a white normal ball
Surrounded by stars, it's like a floating ball far away.

The moon is like a beach ball
It shines like a light during the night.

The moon is like a dime, shining bright
Of course in the night.

Ashleigh Clarke (8)
St Mary's Primary School, Consett

The Beach

The beach is very, very nice.
The sun is gleaming,
The sand is so beautiful and shiny.
There is a lovely glistening sea
The sea washes the sandcastles away.
A big burger stand just sitting there
Shells scattered all over.
Children playing on the sand
Lovely palm trees flowing about.

Shannon Harrop (9)
St Mary's Primary School, Consett

My Rabbit

My rabbit is the best
Gorgeous white with blue eyes
And a small button tail.
My rabbit is the best
Who will snuggle in all day long
She's got the coolest white clothes
So watch out or you could be scratched.
My rabbit is the best
She hides under the paper
So she's the best
Oh my rabbit, you're the best.

Casey Beard (9)
St Mary's Primary School, Consett

Ice Cream

Ice cream, ice cream,
As creamy as can be,
As white as a snowy owl sitting on a tree.

Ice cream, ice cream,
Goes with a pie,
As cool as a cucumber sitting on your eye.

That's why I love ice cream!

Anna McClen (9)
St Mary's Primary School, Consett

Summer

In summer the sun is out
And we run about.
It is very warm,
But watch out for a swarm
Of bees
For these
May sting
If you are irritating.
So maybe it's best
To lie in your vest
And drink a lot of water.

Richard Robinson (8)
St Mary's Primary School, Consett

My Cat

My cat has green eyes
And he never really cries.
He likes to eat
A lot of meat.
He is quite fat,
That's why he lays on the mat.
He looks like he's going to pop,
But that's all right because he's got a Newcastle top.
His whiskers are white and his nose is pink,
That's why he always winks.

Megan Grigg (9)
St Mary's Primary School, Consett

The Moon

The moon is like a shiny large ball
Sitting in the air, opening its wide eyes.

The moon is like a banana
Sitting quietly in the air waiting to be eaten.

Laura Johnson (8)
St Mary's Primary School, Consett

The Moon

The moon is like an enormous light
Shining brightly in the middle of the night.
It sits all alone in quiet space
I wonder how it feels to be stuck up in that old place.

The moon is like a disco ball,
But I really wonder if it can hear my call.
It's like a big smiling face,
Glancing down from empty space.

So that was my poem about the moon
Bye for now, I'll see you soon.

Charlotte Cousin (9)
St Mary's Primary School, Consett

Dolphins

Dolphins always play in the sea,
I wonder how they could stand the cold, lonely breeze.
The dolphins are like cute puppies,
With their cute little faces.

Dolphins always kill sharks
With their long blue noses.
I love the way they 'eek'
With their long blue noses.

Laura Cassidy (9)
St Mary's Primary School, Consett

A Poem About My Cousin Jack

My cousin Jack lay on his back,
Trying to play with a sack,
Even though he's very small,
He likes to play with a ball,
But most of the time
He likes to score a goal.

Anna Siddle (9)
St Mary's Primary School, Consett

Ice Cream

Ice cream is yummy
Ice cream is runny
Ice cream runs down like a stream
So when the sun beams you better hurry
Or you'll be sorry.
All day you take a bite
Ice cream, ice cream sitting in a cone
Ice cream, ice cream cold and fun
Yum, yum, yum.
Ice cream, ice cream in your tum
Ice cream looks like fun, fun, fun.

Jordan Mitchell (9)
St Mary's Primary School, Consett

The Future

The future is so far away,
No one knows what's going to happen.

But I'm sure it will be as noisy as a trumpet
Because of the people.

It will be as crowded as the trees in the forest
There will probably be other life.

The future will be as lively as a cheetah
And to me it will be awesome!

Michael Lilley (9)
St Mary's Primary School, Consett

Marvellous Muggleswick Manor

Muggleswick Manor magically moves mischievously
To the mucky meadow making marks with the mud.

Muggleswick Manor merrily meets
To seek all matters on Mystery Street.

Muggleswick Manor defeats to win
Muggleswick Manor invites all in.

Emily Phillips (9)
St Mary's Primary School, Consett

My Dog

My dog is cute
And silly like me
He's sweet and playful
With a little button nose.
He's got golden fur
With big brown eyes
And he's especially cuddly.
He's always running happily
With his little tail wagging
And that's why he's my dog.

Charlotte Smith (9)
St Mary's Primary School, Consett

All About You

My hamster Tibbles is as compact as a baby shoe,
She is obedient, she is sweet,
She is special to me too.
She has lots of treats and she likes to eat meat,
She likes to sleep in hay,
She has a sleep every day,
She drinks lots of water
And she has a baby daughter.
Tibbles is adorable,
Tibbles scurries around the hall,
Tibbles is white and brown
And she likes to frown,
The kind of hamster my Tibbles is, is a Syrian
And she is worth a billion.

Anna Quinn (9)
St Mary's Primary School, Consett

My Dog Loti

My dog lies beside the fire as if it was hers.
Her lovely coat gleaming as if it was the sun.
Her curled up tangled bed that her big body lies in
Chasing her stubby tail excitedly running around in circles.

With her big pink nose all screwed up and crumpled as a cherry
A big body with her cream and orange coat and big huge paws.
I love her big, long, orange ears that flap around when she runs.
She helps me with my problems,
She is the best at everything.
I love my dog.

Megan Birbeck (9)
St Mary's Primary School, Consett

A Man From Dubai

There was once an eccentric from Dubai,
Who said he looked like a mince pie,
Thick black and red socks,
With brown wavy locks,
But he likes to be beside the sea
And he has legs like the sting of a bee
That obscure man from Dubai!

Rebecca Swinney (9)
St Mary's Primary School, Consett

My Rabbit

My rabbit shines like the light from the stars
That's his name too, Starlight.
He is as silent as a falling feather
Except for when he fights with curtains.

He is so very, very ticklish,
That's what makes him funny.
He is my rabbit,
The funny bunny.

He is small and fluffy,
So, so cute,
As fast as a cheetah,
I'm glad he is all mine.

My rabbit lives in the house,
He actually hates it outdoors,
As nice as a puppy except when he bites
I love him, he loves me.

He loves to eat pellets,
As he hops around the house he will sniff and feel
He plays with me when I am bored
Such a special rabbit.

He was a surprise from my mum
He is a Netherland Dwarf,
So small, he can fit behind my bed
I love him so much, I hope he doesn't leave.

He chews my shoes
He eats newspaper
That my dad leaves on the floor
He is super.

Sophie Milburn (9)
St Mary's Primary School, Consett

My Box

(Inspired by 'Magic Box' by Kit Wright)

My box is made of wool
It is as big as a cat
The shape of my box is like a big shiny star
It opens with a magic enchanted key.
Inside my box are the most precious objects
I'll put a memory of when I do something special
The smell is of cinnamon
The feel inside is like the softest petals
The box closes at sunset
The colour is multicoloured and glittery.

Gabrielle McAleer (11)
St Mary's Primary School, Consett

Christmas

Christmas is coming, presents are waiting
And children are singing Christmas songs.
Mums are buying, dads are helping,
Children are asking, but never to be told.
People are rushing to get early stock for Christmas,
Shop workers are whizzing round to serve everyone in sight.
Night is falling, time is ticking
One minute till Christmas,
People are waking, they shout, 'Alleluia, it's Christmas Day.'
Children waking mums and dads
Children shouting while opening presents
Everybody having a great time
While Santa is getting ready for next time.

Roxanne Ives (11)
St Mary's Primary School, Consett

Fear

Fear is red and black like a stormy night,
It tastes like trickling blood
And it sounds like an axe chopping,
It feels like bumpy gravel!

Anthony Brown (11)
St Mary's Primary School, Consett

Blustery Winds

As destructive as an angry person
Homes being destroyed from all the anger
And I am not smiling,
Thunder and hailstones from the clouds in the sky.
It sounds like an opera singer singing high notes
Like a man stamping around the room.

Christopher Carlin (10)
St Mary's Primary School, Consett

Sweet Shop

The sweet shop that's over the road,
Is my favourite place.
I make the short journey there,
On my pocket money days.

On Mondays I always buy,
Lovely lollipops and yummy sherbet treats.
Followed by a helping of
A gorgeous chocolate feast.

Then on Tuesday
I go there and I just spend,
Spend, spend, until I have
More than I can hold.

The next day,
I'm off again.
Buying sweet sugared jellies
And strawberry candy canes.

And finally I feel sick,
My stomach can hold no more.
I think I'm about to explode
But I can't help it - I want more!

Sophie Page (11)
St Mary's Primary School, Consett

Christmas Night

Angels take flight
Over the kingdom of light
As they are singing
The bells start ringing
On Christmas night darkness falls
Santa starts to hear children's calls.

When the reindeer land
The children demand
Try again because these ones are lame
Today not tomorrow
'Cause hearts are full of sorrow
So please mend our poor hearts today.

Brandon Hicks (10)
St Mary's Primary School, Consett

What Is Love?

Love is sharing
Love is caring
Love is the burning sun
Love is light
Love is kindness
Love is generosity
Love is happiness
Love is sweet music calming me
Love is like melting chocolate
Love is life
Love is stars shining in the sky
Love is like a box of chocolates
Love is secretly special
But most of all love is warmth inside you!

Jayne Donnelly (11)
St Mary's Primary School, Consett

The Monster Next Door

My neighbour next door is called Mrs Arden
I'm sure there's a monster in her back garden!
With bells on its fingers and rings on its toes
You'll notice that monster wherever it goes.

Its head is as big as a helium balloon
To be honest it looks like a great big baboon!
Nobody knows about this monster but I
I won't tell a soul till the day I die.

I can barely go to sleep at night
In case that monster gives me a fright!
I don't want people to think I'm a wuss
My mum and dad, they'll say it's a puss.

You know this monster, it might be OK
But I don't want to find out anyway.
I want to go to Granny Ball's
I'll loose that monster once and for all!

Susanna Quinn (10)
St Mary's Primary School, Consett

Thunder

This morning he woke up and began to *roar,*
His grey world of thunder is a man in a mood,
He cuts off the power
Making ships sway violently across the waves,
The crews' faces as he arrived on the ship,
The crew drowning in the water,
The soldiers in a bad mood,
Making the lions roar,
Making water rise into cities!

Emily Peacock (11)
St Mary's Primary School, Consett

Peacefulness

Peacefulness is like the indigo twilight,
It tastes like a cool breeze.
It smells like a scented rose petal,
It looks like a countryside view.
It sounds like a babbling brook,
It feels like you're in a dream land.

Abbie Spence (10)
St Mary's Primary School, Consett

Don't Be Scared

Fairies, trolls, dragons and dolls, very smelly indeed,
Unicorns, monsters and all those things, no one ever believes.
Believe it or not I've seen the lot!
I've talked to fairies, they're just not scary,
I've talked to trolls, they're awful dolls.

I've seen them in the wardrobe,
I've seen them on the stairs,
I've seen them nearly everywhere
And I'm still not scared.

Witches, wizards, ghosts and elves, very smelly indeed,
Pixies, gnomes, goblins and sprites and all those things.
No one ever believes, believe it or not, I've seen the lot!
I've talked to witches,
They're so not scary.
I've talked to ghosts,
They're awfully smelly.

I've seen them in the wardrobe,
I've seen them on the stairs,
I've seen them nearly everywhere
And I'm still not scared.

So don't be worried, don't be scared,
They're only monsters on the stairs.

Caitlin O'Keeffe (11)
St Mary's Primary School, Consett

My Mam

She makes my tea and she tidies for me
She tidies the house so we don't get mice.

She makes my bed and washes my head
She does the dishes so they don't become vicious.

She makes me look my best
So people are well impressed.

She helps me with my homework
Even though she does all the housework.

My mam is the best mam in the world,
Well I think she is.

Katie Murphy (11)
St Mary's Primary School, Consett

Hate

Hate is grey like a massive thunderstorm.
It tastes like rotten cheese with green mould seeping out.
It smells like a decomposing corpse.
It looks like a war-torn wasteland.
It sounds like one million children screaming.
It feels like being stabbed in the back.

Peter Leech (11)
St Mary's Primary School, Consett

My Friend Danni

My friend Danni is as cute as can be
She is so mini
And she smells like a lily.
She is so funny
I love her like a bunny.
She is as bright as the sun
She is always up for loads of fun
She loves to play in the snow
She has a little pinky toe
My friend Danni is as cute as can be.

Elizabeth Gibson (9)
St Mary's Primary School, Consett

My Fish

My fish are greedy
They have shiny scales that gleam in the sun
They are very fat.
My fish are fast
They do backflips in the water
They are very cheeky.
My fish are smart
My fish are 2 and one is 3
They are always hungry.
My fish can do tricks
And play hide-and-seek
They are my fish.

Tom McClen (9)
St Mary's Primary School, Consett

My Fish

My fish has fins like a whale's tongue
If you mess with him you will be sorry
My fish is loving, just like me
My fish closes his mouth every second
Just like a crocodile, *snap, snap!*
He hides under the bridge watching, just like a dead fish
My fish swims faster than a shark
His name is Fast, Fast is cool, Fast is very fast.
Fast is wicked just like me.
He has a big heart like a football
My fish loves football that is just all he does
All day that is his favourite sport
Just like me he plays football with his stones
My fish, I love you more every single day.

Patrick Brown (9)
St Mary's Primary School, Consett

My Aunty's Dog Bonnie

Bonnie is as happy as a joyful baby
Bonnie has fur as soft as a mattress
Bonnie's ears are floppy as socks
Bonnie's nose is as cute as a black button
Bonnie has soft warm eyes
Bonnie is bright as a light
Bonnie's fur is white as snow
Bonnie always makes me laugh.

Hope Hilditch (9)
St Mary's Primary School, Consett

Meg The Dog

Meg is such a humorous dog
And is always playing.
She is such fun all the time
And never falls out with me.
She is very good at jumping,
Always makes me smile.

She cheers me up when I'm sad
And I always go to see her.
She always plays with me
And oh she is so cute
What a lovely dog she is!

Aimee Simpson (9)
St Mary's Primary School, Consett

Millie My Rabbit!

Millie my rabbit is as cute as can be,
I think she really loves me.

She makes me laugh,
She is warm and cuddly.

Millie my rabbit is as cute as can be,
I think she really loves me.

She hops around her wooden hutch,
She is so enjoyable.

Millie my rabbit is as cute as can be,
I think she really loves me.

She is jumpy and crazy,
She is grey and white.

Millie my rabbit is as cute as can be,
I think she really loves me.

Hannah Roberts (9)
St Mary's Primary School, Consett

My Teacher

My teacher is a cave troll,
Not graceful like a China doll.
She has frog's legs, fingers like pegs.
That's my teacher!

My teacher is so snappy, no way, never happy,
Her ears are like horns
I bet her feet have corns!
That's my teacher!

My teacher is fatter than a hippo,
She has a stupid name, Bippo.
She has a funny hairy tash, her nose is so mashed.
That's my teacher!

My teacher is ever so loud,
Not quiet like a floating cloud.
Her lessons are so boring, everyone is snoring.
That's my teacher!

My teacher is the worst
I'm sure she's cursed.
We can't wait till we leave here.
That's my teacher!

Katie Westgarth (9)
St Mary's Primary School, Consett

The Creature

The creature I know is big and scary,
The creature I know is fat,
The creature I know has thirteen heads,
What do you think of that?

The creature I know is green and slimy,
The creature I know is bad,
The creature I know is very ugly,
But still it's never sad.

The creature I know is tall and strong,
The creature I know is loud,
The creature I know is not a preacher,
The creature I know is my teacher.

Adam Dent (9)
St Mary's Primary School, Consett

Lindisfarne

I love taking walks around the island,
Through the sand dunes on a warm summer's day.
In the spring, riding my bike along the edge of the causeway
Along the harbour on cold winter days
Watching the coloured leaves
As autumn fades away.
Why can't everywhere be like this today?

Hannah Phillips (11)
St Mary's Primary School, Consett

Love

Love tastes like some Roses chocolates,
Love smells like blood-red roses,
Love looks like a newborn baby,
Love feels like hot leather,
Love sounds like your heart beating
Love is the best thing in the *world!*

Rebecca Donnelly (11)
St Mary's Primary School, Consett

Snow

Snow . . . soft white blanket covering the ground,
Under your feet it makes a crunching sound.
Falling from the sky as beautiful as can be,
It's the best scene you'll ever see.
I built a snowman, fat and chubby,
That's the reason I called him Tubby!
I love the snow, I like it deep,
After it snows I can barely sleep.
I love to have snowball fights,
After it's been snowing all night.
It's like a blanket for when the ground goes to sleep
And it won't be touched by anyone's feet.
The trees go from green to perfect white,
It glistens and sparkles under the sunlight.
It's soft to touch and fluffy to hold
But the only thing is . . . I don't like the cold!

Lauren Parker (11)
St Mary's Primary School, Consett

Happiness

Happiness is as yellow as the sun
It tastes like hot fudge melting in your mouth
It smells like salty sea air
It looks like a bed of beautiful roses
It sounds like birds whistling in the morning
It feels like you are having a lucky day!

Andrew Oates (11)
St Mary's Primary School, Consett

War

War is blood-red like boiling scalding lava,
It tastes like charcoal,
It smells like a rotting dead body,
It looks like a foggy dark swamp,
It sounds like crying out in pain,
It feels like being stabbed with a carving knife.

Robert Owens & Oliver Clarke (11)
St Mary's Primary School, Consett

Hate

Hate is grey like a massive thunderstorm.
It tastes like rotten cheese with green mould seeping out.
It smells like a decomposing corpse
It sounds like the Grim Reaper's footsteps
It feels like falling through thousands of feet of holly bushes.

Tom Malone & Jordan Donnellan (11)
St Mary's Primary School, Consett

My Dog Molly

Molly is my dog
She likes the fog
She loves to get dirty
And loves her friend Betty
She is white like snow
She loves it when the light glows
She is very mad
And sometimes very bad
She is very lazy
She loves to eat daisies
She is so cute
And she chews on my boot.

Lucy Hannah Hudson (9)
St William's RC VA Primary School, Trimdon Station

Pets

Pets are little and cuddly
Some like to get muddy
My dog Buster is strong
My mam thinks he is King Kong
He likes a pat
But he is fat
He lays on his back
And falls asleep on my brother's racetrack.

Lauren Mayhew (9)
St William's RC VA Primary School, Trimdon Station

Pets And Friends

I like my friends
I like my pets
At least I don't have to take my friends to the vets
My pets are soft
My friends are kind
But unfortunately my dog is blind
My friends and pets are not the same
My pets run around
And my friends play games
My friends have arms
My birds have wings
But they both give me friendship and that's the thing.

Rebecca Spellman (9)
St William's RC VA Primary School, Trimdon Station

Ronaldinho Kennings

Swift-dribbling
Scored-penalty
Skill-making
Goal-scoring
Match-winning
Brilliant-stunning
Quiet-cunning
Fantastic-heading
Skilful-playing
Award-winning
Great-volleying
Class-striking
Chance-making
Autograph-giving.

Emeka Ononeze (9)
St William's RC VA Primary School, Trimdon Station

Pets!

My pet Bruno runs around the house
But he is not the size of a little tiny mouse
When he sits on your lap he likes to have a little pat
When Bruno is getting fed it will be gone today
He enjoys it but he is not the one that has to pay
When he is in his bed he lays down his little furry head.

Jessica Storey (10)
St William's RC VA Primary School, Trimdon Station

What Is A Pet?

Dogs are a type of pet.
They make you feel happy.
Their tongues have wet patterns.
They feel very sloppy.

Fish are another type.
They go glub, glub, glub.
They need a bit of space
But don't put them in the bathtub!

Cats are my favourite.
I love the way mine purrs.
I have three cats
And they all have different fur.

So what is a pet?
It is something you adore.
I will love my pets forever
And I wish that I had more!

Ciaran Jasper (10)
St William's RC VA Primary School, Trimdon Station

Pets!

Pets, pets, always go to the vets
Hamsters, hamsters, love their food
Hamsters, hamsters, never in moods.

Pets, pets, hate the vets,
Dogs, dogs, jump in bogs
Dogs, dogs, try to catch hogs.

Pets, pets, love the vets,
Cats, cats, like to catch rats
Cats, cats, lie on old mats.

Pets, pets, are all right at the vets
Dolphins, dolphins, swim in water
Dolphins, dolphins have a very strange snorter.

Aimee Elder (8)
St William's RC VA Primary School, Trimdon Station

Cats

Never gets cuter
Claws can't get sharper
Eyes don't get smaller
Nothing jumps higher
Always get better
Cat food can't get stinkier
Can't taste worse
Very fast eaters
Good sleepers
Never softer
Fast runner
Not like a gorilla.

Lorna Hubbard (9)
St William's RC VA Primary School, Trimdon Station

My Nana

My nana is special to me
And to all of our family.

She's always there to give me a love and a hug
And a cup of coffee in my favourite mug.

I love my nana so very much
I love her little gentle touch.

My nana is special as can be
Just like a dolphin swimming in the deep blue sea.

Sophie Fellows (10)
St William's RC VA Primary School, Trimdon Station

Henry VIII Kennings

Wife killer
Sudden thriller
Wedding basher
Love thrasher
Diet hater
Girl dater
Life ender
Low bender
Wine drinker
Quick thinker
Selfish manner
Work banner
Heavy eater
Tough beater
Intelligent boozer
Fat loser.

Sarah Cant (9)
St William's RC VA Primary School, Trimdon Station

Age

Age is a funny thing you know
It increases so quick, where does it go?
First you ride your bike quickly straight ahead
Next thing you know you're mending them in the shed.
Age grows bigger and it's weird because
You start to need glasses and wigs 'cause of hair loss.
Age is like a giant tree
It grows and never gets smaller, see.
As people grow older there's not only their age that will grow
Their minds will become more adventurous and more they will know.

Nicole Peters (11)
St William's RC VA Primary School, Trimdon Station

Who Am I?

Who am I?
I have a snowy white coat
And long sharp claws to catch my dinner
Who am I?

A polar bear.

Who am I?
I have big wide eyes
And I am very wise
I swoop down to catch my prey
Who am I?

An owl.

Vicky Barber (10)
St William's RC VA Primary School, Trimdon Station

Seaside

Sitting on the soft golden sand
Waves crashing in front of me
Seagulls flying high and low
Looking for a snack.

Children playing in the sand
Making sculptures
Little boats, red and white
People in gliders taking flight.

That's what happens
On this lovely beach.

James Slattery (10)
St William's RC VA Primary School, Trimdon Station

Daytime And Night-Time

When the people are awake
Waiting for the moon to break
The trees are swaying all day long
Little birds singing a song
When night-time comes, we go to bed
It's time to lie down your sleepy head.

Megan Grimley (11)
St William's RC VA Primary School, Trimdon Station

Ice

Slipping, sliding on the ice
When you fall over, it's not nice
Having fun in the snow
When it melts the river will flow.

Sliding on the road
Makes a wagon spill its load
Snow and ice are so much fun
Make sure you don't run.

Tom Robertson (10)
St William's RC VA Primary School, Trimdon Station

Try And Guess Who I Am!

Try and guess who I am
I knock people over
And call them names
I sometimes hit and kick them
I make fun of what they look like
So I can have a good laugh.
I am a *bully!*

Try and guess who I am
I get punched and kicked
Also get called nasty names
I am made fun of what I look like
I am the one who stays at home
Pretending that I am ill.
I am the victim of bullying.

Abbie Geldard (10)
St William's RC VA Primary School, Trimdon Station

Birds

Birds singing, soft and sweet
Making not even one tweet
Flying high and swooping low
Down they come to say hello
On the grass they stand eating
While the baby birds are sleeping
When at last they go to their nests
So they can have a big long rest.

Terri Armstrong (11)
St William's RC VA Primary School, Trimdon Station

The Unicorn

Long, long ago, far, far away
A witch chased a unicorn
And this is what she had to say,
'Give me your horn, give it here.'
The evil witch whispered that in his ear.
The unicorn ran as fast as he could
Heading towards the deep, dark wood.
He passed an owl who sang a song
But with a swoop of his horn
The witch was gone.
The unicorn looked and the witch was nowhere near
As he trotted back into town
The unicorn got a great big cheer.

Jenny Harnett (9)
St William's RC VA Primary School, Trimdon Station

Seasons

Baby animals are born in spring
A baby bird will spread its wings
Animals will give a cry of joy
Whether their baby is a girl or boy.

Summer is so hot
It's like a burning oven pot
In summer we have fun
Underneath the burning sun.

Autumn leaves are simply the best
Each one is crunchier than the rest
Red, orange, brown and gold
What colour is the leaf you hold?

Winter trees, tall and bare
Will you see a winter hare
Making footprints in the snow?
Shall we go on our sleigh?
Off we go!

Shannon Turnbull (11)
St William's RC VA Primary School, Trimdon Station

Dinosaur Vs Dragon

Big and hard dinosaurs
Soft and weak dragons
Big footprints
A lot of fire
A lot of burning
Bits of ash
A lot of gas
Very big and very small
No one can escape
A very loud sound
A very hungry monster.

Kallum James (11)
St William's RC VA Primary School, Trimdon Station

A Far Away Town

I had a dream last night
A very exciting dream
I found a new town
Where I would walk where I please
Loads of houses
But not a person in sight
Not a sound or a spark
Not even a light
It is not a real town
That is a shame
To know that when I wake up
It will be all over
Till I go to sleep again.

Matthew Butler (11)
St William's RC VA Primary School, Trimdon Station

The Moonlight Fairy

The moonlight fairy dances all night,
She glows with such a lovely light.

She has a lovely little house,
It's like a palace for a mouse.

The wings of the fairy are so bright,
They even dazzle the sun with their light.

Her powers are so strong,
They have been the greatest for so long.

The moonlight fairy is so small,
You would never notice her at all.

The moonlight fairy dances all night,
She glows with such a lovely light.

Louise Gardiner (11)
St William's RC VA Primary School, Trimdon Station

Friends

Friends are helpful every day
Even when you don't want to play.
They make up with you when you're not kind
And also when you won't change your mind.
Friends are great and also fun
They play with you in the sun.
Friends help you when you're sad
Even when you have been bad.
Overall, friends forgive
And that is why friends are friends.

Thomas Robertshaw (11)
St William's RC VA Primary School, Trimdon Station

Big Dragons

There are dragons in the town
The people are terrified
All around there is screaming
People running
Dragons breathing fire
Setting homes on fire
Dragons stamping through the streets
Knocking down buildings
Dragons staring into the people's eyes
With their red eyes.

Kyle Webb (11)
St William's RC VA Primary School, Trimdon Station

A Sword In A Stone

There once was a sword in a stone
And a poor man who lived alone
Also a very beautiful princess
Who was wearing a gorgeous dress.
The sword parted from the stone and came out
Everybody turned happy and started to shout
The man was a prince and had loads of pride
And the beautiful princess became his bride.

Thomas Barker (10)
St William's RC VA Primary School, Trimdon Station

A Dragon's Tale

I'll tell you the tale of a dragon
A very long time ago
He slept all day and flew all night
Now it's a dragon you wouldn't want to know.

It terrorised the town with its fire-breathing breath
Although it was a lazy dragon, it scared them all to death
Its scaly body slithered around
Making a terribly horrid sound.

Ryan Willis (10)
St William's RC VA Primary School, Trimdon Station

When T-Rex Were It!

Marc Bolan superstar
He sang rock songs and played the guitar.
Marc's success made girls go wild
Especially 'Elemental Child'.

The band T-Rex had four number ones
With all heartbreaking love songs
The poet dazzled people's minds
About lifetime sadness and how he cried.

There was a time everything was fine
Marc was great when he said that line
Something happened that's lost pop's gleam
Whatever happened to the 'teenage dream'?

Rebecca Ashford (11)
St William's RC VA Primary School, Trimdon Station

Alan Shearer

Shearer going down the line,
His shirt number is number nine.
He broke his record with 201 goals,
He always puts it between the poles.

He scores a penalty every time,
He might go for 209.
As a footballer he does just fine,
His boots always shine.

Jordan Lavery (10)
St William's RC VA Primary School, Trimdon Station

Summer Sweet

Summer is beautiful in each and every way,
It is beautiful every day.
People laugh and people play,
Butterflies swoop and butterflies sway.

Summer is fabulous so please don't go,
You shall come back and never say no.
Have a lot of fun
And always think of the sun.

Summer is great,
So don't tempt fate.
So have a brilliant day
And always, always play.

Jane Snowball (10)
St William's RC VA Primary School, Trimdon Station

Day And Night

At night the darkness is bright,
The trees start to whisper and fight.
Cars start to groan and snore
As the moon comes into the sky
The sun says goodbye.

As dawn is broken and day is here,
The grass sings with joy and happiness.
But the night draws near
As the sun lies low
The moon shines high
And slowly the noises begin to die.

Claire Harnett (11)
St William's RC VA Primary School, Trimdon Station

The Springtime

In spring new life is born into the world
The air smells lush and green
The sound of joy lingers
The sound of children playing outside.
The look of spring is delighting new life brought all around
Flowers budding round every corner you turn
Spring tastes fresh and new
It tastes lush and happy.

Spring is the best season
Joy and new life are spread all around
Spring is when life has started
And we all have a new and fresh chance of life.

Jessica Collett (9)
St William's RC VA Primary School, Trimdon Station

Ten Little Trolls

Ten little trolls standing in a line,
One fell down then there were nine.

Nine little trolls eating off a plate,
One didn't have one then there were eight.

Eight little trolls flying up to Heaven,
One got lost then there were seven.

Seven little trolls at the Grand Prix,
One got run over then there were six.

Six little trolls doing the jive,
One slipped over then there were five.

Five little trolls walking through a door,
One walked into it then there were four.

Four little trolls sitting up a tree,
One fell down then there were three.

Three little trolls sitting on the loo,
One fell in then there were two.

Two little trolls sitting on a bomb,
One blew up then there was one.

One little troll at the seashore,
It got washed up then there were no more.

Robbie Morgan (9)
St William's RC VA Primary School, Trimdon Station